i had you in july

By: Kayla French

First Edition, 2025
ISBN (paperback): 979-8-9930269-0-9

Cover photograph: Shirley Ann Gillam, used with family permission.
Cover design, interior layout, and illustrations: Kayla French.

Published by Kayla French Publishing
Printed in the United States of America and other countries
Author contact: ihadyouinjuly@gmail.com
Instagram: @kaylafrenchauthor

10 9 8 7 6 5 4 3 2 1

Before You Begin

This book includes medical trauma, dying, and loss, with references to substance use, organ donation, and suicide. Read in a way that feels safe for you. Please skip ahead to the Resources section in the back for additional support anytime you need.

These pages were written in hospital rooms and through sleepless nights; they aren't tidy, but they're true. If you're here with your own grief, I am so sorry. May these poems help you feel less alone.

This is a memoir. Some names and details have been changed for privacy. This work reflects my experience and is not medical, legal, or therapeutic advice.

If you are in the United States and in crisis, call or text **988** (Suicide & Crisis Lifeline), use chat at **988lifeline.org**, or dial **911** for immediate emergencies.

Dedication

For my Mother, my home.

You believed in me when I couldn't believe in myself. You saw a writer, a voice, a mind worth trusting long before I did.

You gave me my heart, my compassion, the part of me I'm most proud of. I hope I haven't lost that heart, even if I hardly recognize myself right now. I promise to keep fighting for the light, like you always did.

Those three weeks will always stay with me, not only for the pain, but for the closeness. I hope you felt me. If I could choose again, I'd still choose to be there for every minute, the way I know you would have been for me.

Thank you, Mama. Thank you for everything. I miss you so much.

i had you in july

i had you in july

Floor 5
where I slept for weeks
on that flat blue couch in the corner,
short hours at a time,
then rushed into the ICU across the hall
the moment my eyes opened
and I remembered.

This wasn't a dream.
It was the nightmare
we were living.
They buzzed me in.
They stopped asking who I was there to see.
They knew me.
"Come on in, hun."
I'd round the corner.
Take a left.
Bay 1. Bed 1.

And there you were.
I had you.
I watched you.
Game Seven, World Series.
My World Series.
I learned every beep,
clinging to the thought that
knowledge might make the chaos obey.
Maybe if I understood enough,
this room might feel less like
it was swallowing me whole.

I pulled a chair up to your side,
snuggled into your warm skin.
I smelled the hospital pillows,
tuned into the constant beeping.

Norepinephrine.
Epinephrine.
Vasopressin.
MAP: 57.
"Oxycodone, please.
Is she due for her oxycodone?"
Feeding-tube refill.
Intracranial pressure elevated.
Pressure control protocol triggered.
"Hold the nimodipine indefinitely!"
Cardiac arrhythmia.
Occlusion in line.

Occlusion.
Nothing moving forward.

They came in,
pushed you, pinched you.
Do something, Mom.
Fight them back.
And in moments you did.
You withdrew from their
prodding hands.

I spent my life trying to protect you from pain.
There I was,
hopeful, happy,
horrified
to watch.
Because it felt like I had you.

And on day eight you opened your eyes,
but you still seemed
just out of reach.

I had you in July.

But you didn't improve.
Your brain scans,
blurred by blood,
showed potentially more ischemia,
more stroke,
more devastation.

We waited.
Asked for more scans, more opinions, more.
Please just give me a little more.
She deserves more.
She deserved MORE.

We fought.
You fought.

The team of neurosurgeons marched in
almost
omniscient.
If you wanted to catch them,
you had to arrive before dawn.
"We've done everything medically we can.
This is not survivable."

I had you in July.

I had you for 23 days in July.
And now,
now it's August.
I hate its bitter name.
July, like a thread that ties you to me.
August, a knife cutting it loose.
The birds are still chirping.
The flowers you planted still bloom.
How can they keep going?
Don't they know the sun left in July?

I had you in July.

i had you in july

before

i had you in july

wom|b|an

She was my home before I had a name.

mine

My Mom.
I say it like a key,
something I clutch and keep safe.
"She's my Mom too,"
my older sister laughs.

*"I say it like that
when I talk about you, too!"*
"My Sister."
"My Best Friend."
"My Niece and Nephew."
"My Godson, Goddaughters."
"My."

What is it about these names,
these labels I hold so fiercely?
Maybe they're roots,
etched deep into my story,
marking my place,
my claim.

These faces, these names,
I say them proudly.
They are mine.

gone in a hurry

I knew, even then,
the moments I rushed through
were the ones
I someday would give anything
to live again.

moonflowers

She saw them first,
pushing through a crack in the driveway.
To most they were weeds,
something pesky
destined to be crushed.
Not to her.

She drove a wooden post beside them.
Don't run these over.

She knew their truth.
One night to shine, just one.
They open as the moon climbs,
pale, luminous, defiant
faces wide into the dark.
By morning they collapse, gone.

One night was enough to matter.

Beauty is still beauty,
even when it is brief,
even when it is born in harsh places.

She tended blossoms in cracked soil
and they bloomed
because someone loved them
enough to notice.

She was one herself,
a flower that shone against the odds.
A woman who believed in
what could thrive
when no one else expected it to.

i had you in july

could we please start over?

DECEMBER 24, 2024 • 8:28 AM • IMESSAGE
Mama: Could we please start over today? I love you with all my heart… You are the most thoughtful, giving person I know. You deserve to be happy and I really would love for you to have a great day today.

the weight we carry

"You are so mature for your age,"
as if I chose the grown-up shoes
I slipped into too soon.

Little hands held you steady,
swaying under a weight
they struggled to bear.
Those hands grew,
still holding on,
a pull to protect,
a hope things might get better.
They did.
You did.

But even after the storms settled,
my corner stayed dark.
This time, I was the one swaying,
and you held me
steady, strong.

The truth was constant,
wherever we stepped,
we stepped together.
And I would follow you
into fire.

i had you in july

i hate myself

APRIL 26, 2025 • 7:46 PM • IMESSAGE
Me to Sissy: *I put on this mask*
And Mom just loves me.
So it feels safe
to take it off.
But she gets
the worst of me.
I hate myself for it.

Self-awareness without embodiment
is drawing a map of every
dead
end,
every
wrong
turn,
every
cliff,
and still driving off the road anyway.

keith urban concerts

You watch him,
your favorite.
But I watch you.

The best sound,
I always tell you this,
your laughter.

Coffee on a blanket at the park,
you braid my hair
and I watch the woolly bear caterpillars crawling,
the same ones from my childhood.

Hand hearts beneath the Northern Lights,
coastal air and Redwood trees,
escape room victory with seconds to spare,
keepsakes collected of our breaths.

Lost and tired under a pile of flashcards *we* study for the
National Counselor Exam.
I passed.

You often bring me surprise flower bouquets from
your garden and tell me,
"A job I would like is making flower arrangements."
Your flower arrangements are beautiful.

You pick up the grandkids on early-out Fridays,
show off the new pots you thrifted for your plants.
We stash away dollars for that family trip…
the one we've been saying
we are long overdue for.

We dream, we plan, we imagine
the days
with you in them.
All of them.

i had you in july

dull headache

APRIL 14, 2025 • 10:04 PM • IMESSAGE
Me: *Thank you for helping me when I was sick this morning and for dinner and for bringing those things. For drying my hair. You're the best Mom.*
Mama: You're so sweet! You're the best! Love u. Just achy and a dull headache.

out of time

"I think you've been doing too much.
Maybe you should slow down.
Your leg cramps at night are bad,
maybe you just need to rest a little more."

She looked at me,
eyes glistening with something I couldn't name.

"I've wasted so many years of my life.
I don't want to waste another second."

And so, she didn't.

i had you in july

awake and invisible

I remember my Mom told me
about a time she woke up mid-procedure.

The anesthesia wasn't right, and
she could hear.
She could feel.
And the dentist didn't notice
she was awake.

That was her worst nightmare,
being awake
and invisible
at the same time.

in full bloom

Sun-kissed shoulders,
side ponytail and
oversized scrunchie with
hands buried in the soil.
She knows exactly
where to press,
where to loosen.
The flowers leaned into
her.
I think they know,
she was
the reason
they bloomed.

i had you in july

five days before

She walked me slowly
through her flowers,
naming each one
like an old friend.

I stopped to take photos.
"You're so good, Mom."
I told her,
and her smile bloomed
right there among the roses.

Zoom out, I thought.
Don't just take a picture of her flowers,
take a picture of her
in her flowers too.

And in that millisecond
a **shadow** flickered,
the same one
always waiting.
It comes in our fights
and in the sweetness
of something ordinary.

You won't have your Mom
forever.

Have you ever wondered
which picture
would be the last one
you ever take of someone?

June 28th, 2025

last text

Mama: Love you. Proud of you!!!

i had you in july

during

i had you in july

read the room

I have spent my whole life
watching.
Signs.
Body language.
Breaths.

They call it a *trauma response.*
If you can read the signs,

maybe

you can stop the worst thing from happening.

So, when the doctor scanned the room for the stool,
I already *knew.*

"No," I cry.
"No!"

She sat down next to us,
intentionally eye to eye.

"This is a catastrophic brain bleed."

There it was.
My worst thing.

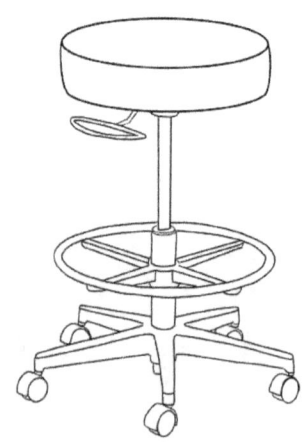

away

Bye Mom! I'll see you soon, Mom!
I yell. I watch.
You're in the sky.
Up, up, and
away.
They agreed to take you.
There was brainstem function!
A faint glimmer of
hope.
You fly off to a
"Level-1 world-renowned trauma center,"
the very same place I graduated from,
with honors,
with pride,
Iowa.
Home.
The Hawkeyes.
Today
I see that same hawk
but different,
descending from the sky
silent, swift,
a shadow that steals you
away.

first sleep

There are so many lasts now,
and too many firsts.
I knew I was different.
Changed.
When I realized I hadn't slept in three days.
I texted Sissy,
 "I don't want to go to sleep.
 The last time I went to sleep,
 I still had my Mom."

aggressive

A large central bleed,
white-hot at the midline.
Blood in the ventricles.
An emergency ventriculostomy
to relieve pressure in your brain.

Most don't make it
to the hospital at all.
You did.

"But with Hunt–Hess 5,
and a GCS this low,
our expectations
are very, *very* reserved.
We usually like to see
more improvement first,
but another team will come by
to talk about
whether you'd want to proceed
with aggressive coiling.
It would be your best chance
to prevent re-rupture,
but it doesn't repair
what's already been lost."

Do it.
Mom made it here.
Most don't,
but she did.

Let's be aggressive.
Let's give her
the best chance
at fighting this.

whispers

I loved you in whispers
where you deserved thunder.

In every goodbye,
I now search for signs,
for proof you knew,
You were my entire universe.

I loved you too quietly.
On guard watching for danger,
shadows of resentment
woven through the spaces
where we leaned,
both clutching, learning to live.

I whispered apologies
for impatience, for coldness,
for me.

And you forgave.
I forgave you too.

But whispers don't leave echoes like thunder does.
And I wonder if you ever heard me
the way I meant for you to.

Forever your child
quiet in the doorway
making sure your chest still moved,
the air still found you.
But a year into your sobriety,
I found myself
forgetting to watch.

A gift.

You found your light
and I rage at my darkness
for stealing what might have been
our greatest joys.

You carried me through then.
Still, my deepest fear whispered always
losing you.

So why did I love you in whispers
when you always deserved the storm?

hope vs. steel

"The procedure was successful.
We didn't have to open her skull.
Now we wait,
watch for vasospasms,
hope her exam
begins to change."

I held onto hope
that this might be enough.

Still, their words clawed at me,
echoing in the room…
"Understand,
we don't typically see a good prognosis
with bleeds like this."

But just last week,
she walked nearly 20,000 steps
I tell anybody who will listen.

She has so much vitality.
She has lived through so much.
She is so strong.

My hope,
fragile, warm, human,
pressing against
their statistics,
cold steel,
leaving me bleeding.

decibels

On tiptoes
I reach,
carefully around
the ventilator.

The warmth of your ear
presses against my lips.

I shout,
"Mom."
"MOM!"

I pinch your skin,
then pinch my own,
to feel
what you feel.

I bruise,
but not like you.

A steady stream of hands
constantly touch and prod you.

"Menace."
Sissy rolls her eyes, looks away.
"Mom, she's a menace."

"I love you, Mom.
I'm here, Mom.
We're here, Mom."
I'm yelling.
Dying for decibels
to reach you.

"We're here, Mom,"
Sissy whispers softly.

scrub, rinse, repeat

This body insists on rhythm:
bite, swallow, breathe.
I follow orders
scrub, rinse, repeat.

But every motion betrays me.
I should be with you,
not here.

With you.
Where are you?

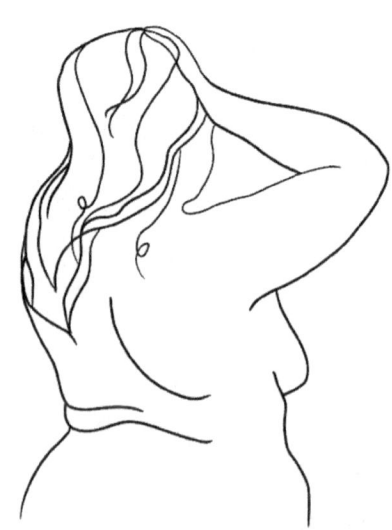

one big sad sleepover

One big sad sleepover.
I say it facetiously,
making my bed in the corner.

Nobody is here for anything good.
Plastic chairs and
pull-out couches,
families gathered in shared silence,
learning to live together in the
Neurosurgical ICU Family
"Lounge."
Where hope and fear breathe the same air.
Strangers united by sorrow.

One early morning,
I see her and I know instantly,
a mother.
Her eyes vacant,
while ten feet away,
he paces on his phone,
his voice cracking through the quiet.

"Are you sitting down?
 He shot himself."

At one point,
we cross the hall together,
waiting to be let into the patient rooms.

He looks at me, "We just lost our 19-year-old."

What do you say to that?
What do you say?

the best grandma

"I miss Grandma."

"Hey, come here.
Sit by Aunt KK.
Tell me, what are you missing the most about Grandma?
I'll play this video for her."

The kids have basically lived in this
waiting room lately,
knowing Grandma is very sick, but
not yet *how* sick.

"Her cheese,"
my seven-year-old nephew says.
"She gets really good presents for us,"
my eight-year-old niece says.

"She does have really good cheese and presents.
Is there anything else you want to say to her?"

"That she's the best grandma,
and I would never, ever want another one."

july 5th

"Come on, let's get you outside,
let's go for a walk."

On cue the skyline is swallowed in
bursts of flames.
My friend called it a great show.

I called it a reminder,
even the brightest lights
fade to ash.

pinpoint

They use a scale
invented by neurosurgeons from
Glasgow, Scotland, and
score you on three things:
Eyes. Verbal. Motor.

Fifteen is perfect.
Six is the best yours has been.
Three is the floor.

Anything below eight…
severe brain injury,
coma,
medical intervention likely required to sustain
life.

I didn't know any of this
until I had to.

They pressed into your sternum,
hard,
watched for a flinch.
They pinched
under your arm,
inner thigh,
drove a pen into your nail beds.
Or
scissors.
Whatever hard thing they could find.

They said it was reflex.
Peripheral, not central.
Peripheral means maybe your spine remembered.
Central means maybe *you* did.

They wanted to see you localize to pain
not just withdraw,
but reach for it, push it away.

That would have been central.
That would have meant *something.*

Your movements were small.
Less than small.
Not absent, but not convincing
enough.

So, we watched for other signs:
Cough. Cornea. Gag.

I said them like scripture,

Cough. Cornea. Gag.

Three points of contact.
Three chances to believe.

I asked about your pupils.
"How's her gaze?
Oh, they were both upward?
Were they equally reactive?
Pinpoint, about two millimeters?"

Pinpoint.

I tried to pinpoint all of it
speak their white coat dialect,
as if understanding would save you
or me, from this
helplessness.

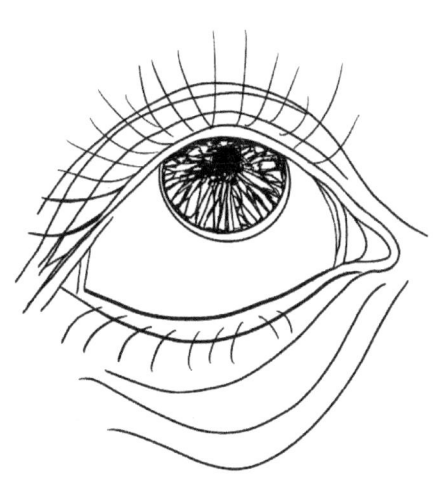

channel 109

I played a lot of music.

Carrie Underwood,
Keith Urban,
Little River Band,
hoping something familiar
might carry her back.

But often I found myself reaching
beyond comfort songs,
reaching for
other frequencies…
Damaged Brain Healing & Nerve Regeneration,
432Hz Super Recovery.

Or

Reliably,
channel 109 on the hospital TV,
spilling galaxies accompanied by
a fuzzy hum of
instrumental music
through the speaker
attached to her bed.

One morning a neurosurgeon found me
half-asleep at Mom's side.
"Keep playing this music, it's good for her."

From then on, I made sure.
I wrote it on the board.
Please leave music on.

Sissy would groan.
"Get that shit off. Can't we watch TV?
Doesn't Mom like murder mysteries? She likes shows."

True.

"Okay, okay. Law & Order. Here."
"He pistol-whipped her and shoved her into the car—"
"Okay, no."

I kept flipping
until I landed on *Family Feud,*
Steve Harvey's voice filling the room.
Laughter echoing from
another world.

When Sissy left,
I turned the galaxies back on.

In the soft hum of space,
I pictured us
floating somewhere in that expanse,
weightless,
unhooked from all the wires and beeping.

Together.

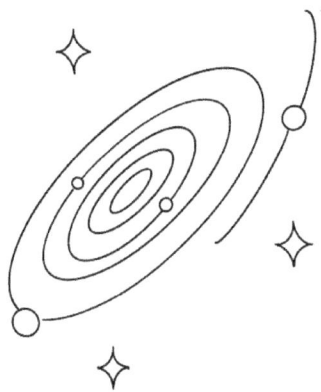

i had you in july

beep

"She's off sedation…"
They'd say,
day after day
as though the words themselves
could open my eyes
to what I could not see.

You had drifted far,
and it seemed like they
thought you should be here,
by now.

Come on, Mom.

With every moment,
heartbreak arrived.

Beep,
after beep,
after beep.

tangled

"Did they shave all the way down?"

"I'm not sure. Let's see.
Oh.
She's got so much hair back here.
But it's matted…
Hey, maybe in an hour or so,
we could wash it?"

Earlier I had asked
her
after asking others,
many times,
"Can we try to get these rings off?
This bracelet?"

The swelling was getting worse.

"This can't be comfortable."

"Let me see who I can contact.
I'm always up for a side mission."

I had learned that what I prioritized for Mom
and what they prioritized for her
weren't always the same.

And I clung
to what made her
human.

I knew
how she would take
scissors to the collars of her shirts
because she hated the feeling
of anything
too tight
around her.

She came back later with
hospital detangler,
baby shampoo,
and a black comb.

She helped make Mom comfortable.
She helped make *me* comfortable.

Spending nearly an hour,
carefully detangling each strand,
making space
not just in my Mom's hair,
but for my own broken being.

In that moment,
for the first time *since*,
I felt a fragile peace
held together by
patience
and the simplest acts
of love.

And
she got the jewelry off, too.

I'll never forget you, M.

weather the weather

Each room held a storm,
hurricane, blizzard, fire…
grief
every
time.
I begged the walls,
I'll take any storm but ours.

i had you in july

maybe i'm selfish

"You have to try to think for your Mom."

Everyone
asks me this question,
"What would she *want* for herself?"

Ugh.
It depends on
everything.

If she could return to
her garden and
lemon cookies and
her children and
sunshine days…

She would want to fight.

If she could come back
to anything like herself,
even slowly,
even less…

Yes.

And
if the path was long,
if the light was dim
but *hers,*
I'd follow.
I would give years.
Drop everything.
Try to help her heal,
if there was hope.
I could carry a long road.
I could carry less of her.

"Think what your Mom would want…
not what you would want."

parking pass it on

"Hi, I couldn't help but overhear
your conversation.
I'm really so sorry for what
you're going through. Hey,
I wanted to let you know
there are parking passes available.
I'm going to give you one.
You can buy a book of them,
and instead of paying $30 a day,
you can pay $8 a day if you get one.
And again, about your Mom, I'm sorry.
But hey.
Just remember,
there are worse things in life than dying."

medicare?

"If you want her to stay alive
like this
to only blink her eyes,
maybe wiggle her toes…

Hospitals have rules.
National rules.
About ventilators.

Fourteen days, then…

You'd be looking at
a brain shunt,
a PEG feeding tube,
a tracheostomy,
a specific and specialized care center.

Medicare will pay
for most of the first two months,
but after that,
the cost will be as much as
over $800 a day."

I pull up my calculator
and stop.

I was never any good at math,
but I knew the answer to this equation.

My salary does not cover the price
in a system
where dollars are worth more than dignity.

home

"Just get out of these walls
for a bit, you know?
Maybe go home for a night."

Don't they get it?
Home is not a place.

chicken or beef?

"We talked about it.
She wouldn't want to live like
this,"
Dad said.
Again.
"With tubes."

And this.
This was tubes.
So
many
tubes.

We
decided
on day eight
to go with comfort care.

Decided.

They asked
like it was a choice
between
chicken or beef.

dnr

"She's full code…"

Noticeable silence.
Sideways glances.
Morning rounds.

We would eventually come to understand
another
cardiac arrest
would bring you back
even
worse.

At the cost of someone
jumping
up
and
down,
breaking
your ribs
to keep you
here.

DNR.

The next day,
I skipped morning rounds.

I couldn't bear to hear them say,
let her go,
when I still felt myself
holding on.

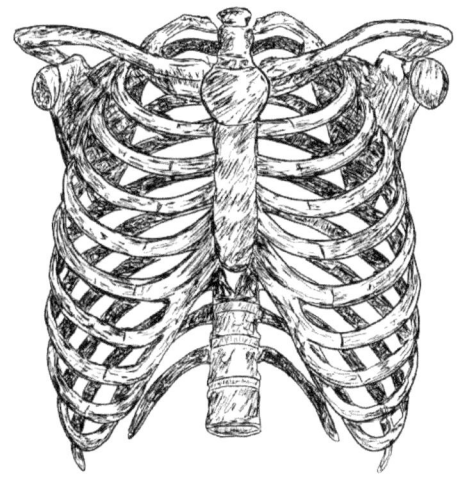

i had you in july

day eight

JULY 10, 2025 • 11:32 PM • IMESSAGE
Me: *She opened her fucking eyes for me.*
Sissy: Shut it.
Sissy: Tell me.
Sissy: Now.

We knew she would do it.
Fight her way back and change up the plan.
That was so her.
She was strong.
Stubborn.
In a way that feels almost impossible to describe…
unless you've
seen how she lived.

"This changes everything for me," Sissy said,
my big sister, who
recently had seemed
so small.
Fragile.
Not invincible the way I needed her
to be while my world was splitting
in two.

I didn't want to tell her
what
I
saw
in Mom's eyes.

How,
from the first time she opened them and on,
she looked *past* me.

How, the second time,
I saw her sadness.

How, the third time,
I met her gaze with pure love and adoration
while she blinked slowly at me for over a minute.
And I prayed,
longed,
for her to see me.

I didn't want to tell her
that every time her eyes opened,
aching fear and longing twisted together inside me
tight,
impossible to separate.

And I really didn't want to tell her that
I knew then,
those brief moments would haunt me forever.

half price, half holding on

"I picked a cremation center. The one in Silvis is half the price."

*"Dad, I can't.
Mom…
Mom opened her eyes last night.
I can't hear you talk about—"*

"Well, I need to talk about it."

I cover my ears
like a little kid.

I'm
not
listening.

Mom opened her eyes.

a to b

"But her Glasgow Coma Scale improved.
She opened her eyes.
It's a seven now!"

"Eye opening can often just be
reflexive…
She's been off sedation for more than ten days now.
Signs of a
positive prognosis would include
purposeful
movements.
Her brain waves remain slow and
abnormal."

"But we moved up on the scale.
We moved up.
Isn't that improvement?
Could this be the scaffolding?
A bridge?
Maybe she just needs more time."

"Her brain is very damaged."

"Okay, so maybe she will never be able to go from A to B again, but,
neuroplasticity, right?
Maybe she could go from A to D to C to B?
Right?
Right…"

too late for questions

I search your skin.
A map with no legend.
My eyes find a long
scar.
What happened here?
I take inventory.
What I asked.
What I didn't.
What I thought time would hold.
Questions pin my ribs.
I keep not knowing.
It keeps me.

tattoo

We had just said it out loud,
after years of
only talking.
We would get the tattoos.
Matching.

For Mom.
A hummingbird.
Her constant devotion,
their wings, daily, at her windows.

We were scrolling through designs
when I opened my wallet,
just reaching for my card.
And then.
Gold.
A flash.
A shimmer.
I froze.
Pulled it out slow.
Hummingbirds.

Card seals.
What the actual.
How were they in there?
When did they get there?
Why didn't I see them until now?
Sissy leaned over.
"What's that?"
"…Hummingbird stickers," I said,
staring like they had just fallen
out of the sky.

Like She had placed them there herself.

ripple

"Wiggle your toes."
Our voices begging.

Sometimes,
after a stillness
you did.

A flicker.

Later,
the nurse said,
"I saw it too."

I asked,
"Could it be reflex?"
"Yes. It can be."

Not always.
Not proof.
But when we asked
sometimes,
sometimes,
a beat later,
there you were.

Hope,
small as a ripple,
rising through your toes,
into our hearts.

another scan?

"Since an MRI
can often get a better look
at tissue,
maybe we can try that too?

I know the brain
can't stitch itself
back together,
but it's remarkable,
isn't it?

You've heard the stories…
how other regions step in,
reroute,
rescue.

Or

what about an fMRI?
I've heard those can
see blood flow?"

"You must be conscious
for that kind of scan.
I can ask neurosurgery,
maybe another CT.
I don't see why they wouldn't
agree to an MRI,
but based on her neuro exam…
this isn't the path
we hoped for.
You see,
this white here?
That…
that shouldn't be there."

i had you in july

"But this is the old scan, right?
Before the drain,
before
bags filling to the brim with
blood,
with
cerebrospinal fluid.
Maybe it's changed.
The drain made room for
healing, and
we can see again.
Please,
let me see again.
You don't know
her strength.
If anyone can
do this,
it's her.
Just...
please
maybe this time
something is
different."

8:00 am • rounds

I hurry in across the hall,
you are so warm.

But your smell has changed.
Not like you,
like,
this place.

I've stopped asking so many questions.
There's only so many ways they can say
the same thing,

"This is a really, really bad brain bleed…"

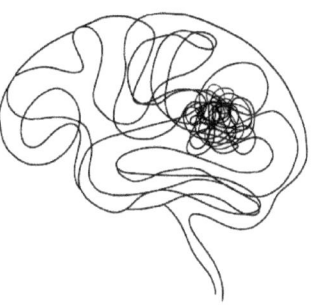

i had you in july

what i couldn't say

"She was supposed to be here.
She was supposed to be here for those things.
She was going to see me do those things, I was going to be…"

My breath falls short and I can't say,
Happy.

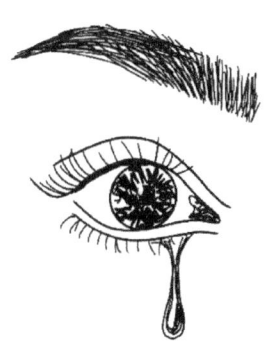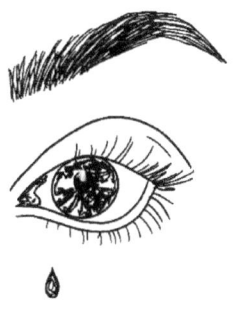

i had you in july

fired

"Hi! I'm her daughter,
I'd just like to help, however I can.
Can I help switch these boots?
Do we switch every two hours?"

"I've been a critical care nurse for thirty-three years."

"Oh. Okay... I just ask a lot of questions.
It's how I try to hold
a little control
in this chaos."

Absence felt dangerous but
my skin itched with neglect.

"I'll be right back, Mom,
I need a shower.
I love you."

After three days
I learned the water wasn't cold,
just user error.
Sometimes I left it cold anyway,
trying to shift the pain from
the elephant on my chest.

I rushed back to her.
Gently reached for her face,
stroked her shaved hair,
soft stubble growing in.

"Hi, Mommy."

"Don't."

Like a whip.
"You can't touch her there."

Not care.
Control.
I jumped,
scolded,
a kicked dog.

*"I have been here
for ten days,
all but
crawled into bed beside my Mom
under rotating care teams and neurosurgeons.
Nobody once told me
don't
touch
her."*

I didn't touch the bandage.
Didn't graze the drain.

She snapped at the nearness of my hands,
as if what I carried
was a toxic, contagious infection,
not tender, heartbroken affection.

"I think I'd like to switch nurses."

notes on a dry erase board:

Discharge Date/Comments:
* Don't forget chapstick *
* Mouth moisturizer please! *
* Keep music on please! :) Ch. 109 *
* Elevate arms *
* Extra pillows! *
Thx for all you do!!!

enough

The updated scan arrives.
Blood clouds the images.
The damage makes everything hard to read.

A drain tunnels into bone,
a coil glimmers at the bomb site.
Possible ischemia
tissue death spreading,
more of her gone,
the kind of injury that can leave a person
an
empty
shell.

At the bedside, her exam shifts.
She isn't as responsive.
Something is pulling her further away.

"So what do I do?
Are things worse?"

Neurosurgeon, Dr. M, replies,
"If you want to see
if she could be that
one in a million…
we can,
but I think
she has suffered
enough."

parts

"Her kidneys are viable.
She could save two lives.
She was a registered donor."

And

"When
would you like us to
remove the ventilator
while you watch her
starve for air,
so we can
take her
working parts
and give them to
somebody else?"

Is what I hear.

hear & here

"I don't care about anything, Mom,
from our past. Okay?
I love you.
I forgive you.
Anything. All of it.

You did good, Mom.
So good.
You need to know how good you are,
how thankful I am you're my Mom.
I would never, ever pick another Mom.

I'm sorry.
I'm sorry.
You deserved more.
I tried, Mom.
I really tried.
I'm going to keep trying.

I want to say I'll be okay,
but it's going to be so hard without you.
Can you hear me, Mom?
Wiggle your toes if you can hear me.
Can you wiggle your toes?

I'm scared.
I'm so scared, Mom.
But I'm not leaving.

I'm here.
I love you.
I'm proud of you."

what i can and can't take home

I sneak flowers into
the sterile, cold
Neurosurgical ICU
no-flower zone.
You deserve flowers.

I quietly tuck one
into your hand,
behind your ear.

After they wilt,
I press them
into the biggest book I can find
from the box of donated volumes.

I record the sound of your heartbeat.
I make prints of your finger,
of your hand.

I can't take you
home.

So I beg
to carry
every
fragment
I can.

delaney kay

"Are miracles real?" she asks.
"I can ask God to
make my Grandma better."

Her eyes hold hope.
Ours hold
the weight of prayers
that never came true.

deliberate

"We've scheduled the operating room for 7:00 PM.
If you want, we can do an
Honor Walk,
doctors, nurses, your loved ones
lining the halls,
before she goes in.

It's a beautiful thing she's doing,
giving—"

*"I'd like to bathe her,
and put a fresh braid in her hair."*

I ask Dad,
bring your flowers from your garden,
each petal
a whisper of your hands
tending to
life.

Sissy cuts them carefully,
and I weave your flower crown
each
strand
devastatingly
deliberate.

You look beautiful.
They all would say it
just how beautiful
you are.

questions to ask the anesthesiologist

- How do you check for air hunger
- Frequency of Morphine
- Do you give anticholinergics for secretions
- Benzo / Ativan, Haldol ??

"Even if she can't respond,
I want to be sure
she isn't anxious,
isn't in pain."

"…Yeah, I'd prefer if you didn't text."
The doctor says a little too flippantly,
a little too light.

"What? No—
I'm writing down what you said."
I point to the filled note in my phone.

Sissy echoes,
"She's not texting."

I haven't slept.
I'm trying to remember everything.
I am begging not just for answers,
but
for
kindness.

This is not routine.
It is my Mother's last moments.
The only chance I have
to speak for her.
If I lose the words,
I lose my last chance to stand
between her and the hurt.

i had you in july

+new playlist

(P)ersonal (P)rotective (E)quipment.
Check.

Dad roars with laughter at me and Sissy in our
stark white jumpsuits.
Says we look like "Ghostbusters."
I haven't heard him laugh like this,
maybe ever.

Hysteria.

In the dark and cold operating room,
it started as the three of us,
but Dad couldn't stay.
He said he was going to
puke.

So
me and Sissy
sat there on those same stools
that *one doctor* pulled up
when she first told us,

"This is a catastrophic brain bleed."

They told us each center does it differently.
This one would give us
ninety
minutes
after removing life support
before they had to
begin.

We watched
them remove
all support…
the same support
that was
crucial in

keeping
you
here,
with us.

We held you, and each other.

*"You are so loved.
You did good, Mama."*

We sang to you.
And they gave us the option
to select songs.
And I did…
I selected
some
songs.

But if the average song is
three minutes long,
I would have needed to select
around
one thousand,
nine hundred,
and
seventy-two
more songs
to play
until
I
would
watch
your
final
breath.

i had you in july

high and headed to hospice

A final offering.
Her kidneys,
giving life.
And she would.
She'd give anyone
anything.

The fine print:
some survive extubation with no support.

Hours earlier,
you were on
so much support.
Even with everything,
they thought
you might go,
"Any minute."
And now?

We reach the waiting room.
"Wait,
she didn't donate her kidneys?"
They all look at us, silent.

"No.
If she makes it a few more hours,
we'll move
to seventh floor, to hospice."

Dad tears up.
"Ohhh no…"

I think he had made peace
with one kind of ending,
the kind where,
someone else is saved
from this Hell.

The kind where Mom is remembered
not for leaving,
but for saving.

But me?
I selfishly just wanted
to see you.

And for a second,
I felt…
High?
A rush.

Maybe
you didn't need all that support.
Maybe
you'd fool them all.
Maybe,
just maybe,
we'd get you
back.

night sweats

The thing about getting high
is you always
come down.

sticky

I kissed your lips,
and sometimes,
your mouth folded
into mine.

A primitive reflex, they said,
the body remembering
what the mind could not.

But my heart
snagged,
caught.

Something clung there,
a sticky hope
that you still knew,
that love could cross
this distance
to reach me.

if only dignity was a language they taught on duolingo

In twenty-one days, I learned a new language,
Mom's silent pain language.
A heart rate change, a grimace, the flicker of her eyes.
The Glasgow Coma Scale became my Bible.

I went from begging her to fight,
hold on.

To questioning,
Why are animals given mercy
while she lay
waiting,
rattling,
caught between
here and gone?

Fuck cautious.
Fuck conservative.

I demanded more morphine,
watching her collarbones climb toward her ears,
each breath sharper, harder.

"Higher doses. Increased basal drips. Add pushes.
More frequently."

"I'll try to come that often, but I could be busy or in a procedure."
And,
"It could be hours until the doctor approves, and the pharmacist makes
the concentration."

"Baby steps," they called it.
Bullshit, I called it.

group chat

Love threaded
through glowing screens.
Food when I couldn't eat.
Check-in after check-in
when my silence was too loud.
Miles traveled
to stand beside me.

Riding the rise and fall
of hope, of despair.
They carried the weight.
They did not flinch.
They stayed.
And I will not forget.

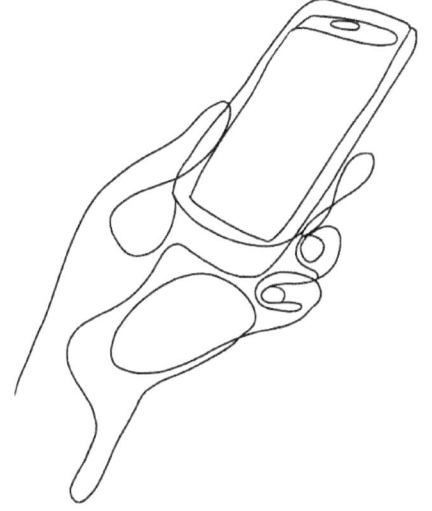

i had you in july

one hundred songs left

A familiar kindness in scrubs
at the door,
the first nurse we met,
back after four days.
I held onto her kindness.
Mom wasn't her patient today,
but she came by anyway.

Wide-eyed,
she
pointed.
"Damnnnnn.
Your
MOM."
All I could say,
"I know.
I know.
My
Mom."

Four days
without life support…

My Mother's strength
made me proud and
simultaneously
terrified me,
a disguise for something cruel,
something keeping her
from peace.

i couldn't save you this time

"I'm scared.
I'm so scared I messed up.
I'm scared I made the wrong choice."
I break.

Dr. L of neurosurgery, a rare presence, sat next to me,
steady,
clear.

"You did not make the wrong choice.

From the beginning
we told you
this was
not
survivable.
But you decided to fight.

We did everything
medically we could.

You have been by her side,
24/7.
You advocate
for her
again, and again.

You are an amazing daughter.

This is just
something incredibly unfortunate
that happened.

I know you can't be objective.
And if it was my Mom,
I couldn't be either.

And I am your least favorite person

right now.
But if it was my Mom,

I would have made
the
same
decision.

This is not you.
This is nothing you did.
This is a
horrific brain bleed.

And
we
have
tried
everything."

whiplash

They tried to prepare me for it.
"It might look like this."
And,
"Just because the
r a t t l i n g
is loud
doesn't mean she's in distress."

Four days on the cot with
tissues shoved tightly in my ears as if
something as delicate as paper
could ever be enough to quiet this
roar.

I tried to muffle the sounds,
sometimes even shut my eyes,
seeing you like *that*,
knowing what each breath meant.

But I
couldn't
be
anywhere
else.
I held you.

And when I saw
it,
I knew instantly.

Those slight,
helpless,
gasps

I knew.
I knew you.

I screamed for my friends,

the two who had bravely stayed with me that night
through these terrifying hours.

"Get a nurse!"

I needed someone,
anyone,
who could check.

But I didn't need them to tell me.
I knew exactly
what was happening.

"All the nurses are busy right now."
"God. Dammit!"
I yelled up at the stark white ceiling.

"Mom. I'm here. I love you."

I never got used to the
whiplash.
Going from
ICU's constant monitors and emergency codes
to only once-daily vital checks…
to what felt like
everyone was
no longer worried about you,
no longer worried about my world.

And by the time the nurse eventually came,
you were gone.

And what poured from me was
pure terror,
hollow sadness,
a rage clinging,
drowning me.

I wanted so badly
to be safe for her,
to be calm for her,

to be strong for her.

I fucked this up.

"I'm here, Mom.
I'm here. I love you."

"I told her that,
didn't I?"

I turned to my friends.

"You told her," they said.
"You were right there."

i had you in july

after

this is my Mom. (until the very end.)

It took 96 minutes
for the neurosurgeon to arrive,
and say what I already knew.

Then it took another 118
for someone to arrive
to tell me they were ready
to take you to the mortuary

long after your skin had turned
that patchy, sickly yellow,
after your blood had gone cold,
after I felt
the stiffness creep into your fingers
as I tried,
softly, secretly,
to stretch them,
to interlace with them,
as if this could stop the process.
Stop all of this.

"In all my years here,
I've never had a mortician take this long,"
the nurse said.

"She's so cold,
her hands are already stiff.
This is my Mom.
This is my MOM.
And I'm not leaving her
until the very end.
I'm not leaving."

I'm torn between
begging them to
show some urgency
and
hoping they never come,
never take you away from me.

I picked a few flowers from a bouquet,
tucked them into your hair,
and told you again and again
how sorry I am.

"You have nothing to be sorry for,"
my friend said as she left the room.

"I'm so sorry,"
I whisper to you again.

"Whenever you're ready."

My mind knows
it's time to
let
go,
but my heart
clings to your hand.

For the last time,
I touch you.

"I hope I'll see you again.
I love you.
I'm proud of you."

The hallway stretches,
shadowed, hollowed,
and I say to them,

"This is my Mom…
And she was a really good Mom…
So
please
be gentle with
Her."

"Of course," they say.

i had you in july

I look back
and know,
for the rest of my life,
I will always keep looking back
for you.

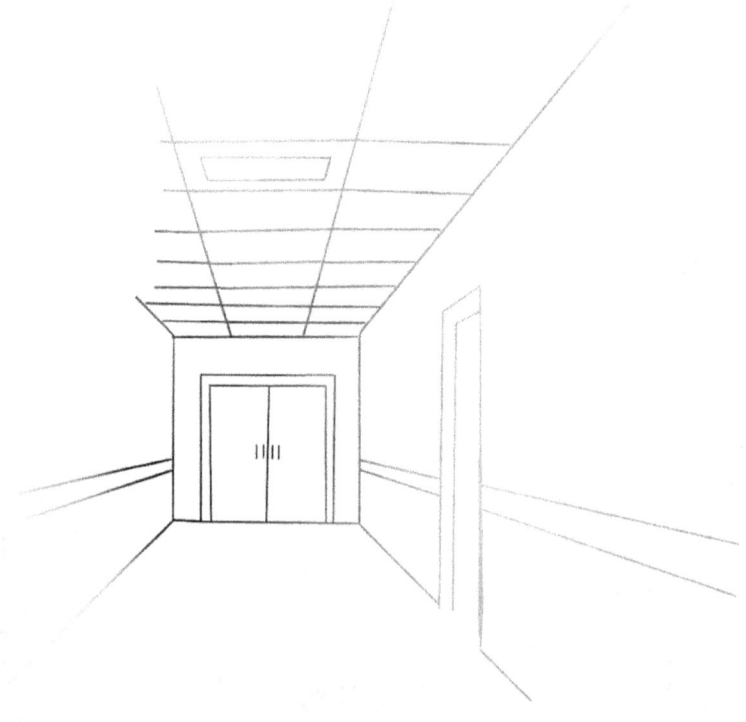

crumbs

They talk about
sudden and unexpected death,
and
anticipated death.

Lucky us
to have both.

Two anniversaries.
Two dates where I feel
like I lost you.

I lost your laugh, your words, your voice
in one single instant.

Then,
for twenty-one days,
there was a drawn-out,
suffocating
knowing, awareness, being,
starved of
you.

Only
toe twitches and eye-flicked crumbs
keeping me barely alive,
until the torturous realization
that my life source
was gone.

both

The thing about sudden death is
there's no goodbye.
No questions asked.
No warning.
You didn't get a say
in the choices we were forced
to heartbreakingly make for you.

And

The thing about anticipated death is,
you live with the ache of waiting,
fear like a slow burn,
watching everything you love
unravel in slow motion.

And the thing about what happened to you,
and to us,
is that it was both.

hiraeth

I am so homesick
for a place I know
I will never
be able to return.

i had you in july

hair

I found my first haircut,
a small,
scattered tuft of hair between tape,
tucked into the pages
of a partly filled baby book.

It feels ironic.

After they placed the drain
into the ventricles of your beautiful mind,
they shaved your hair,
swept it into a bag,
and I knew I had to keep it.

You saved my first,
and I saved your last.

Another quiet whisper of love,
though maybe whispers
aren't so quiet after all.

the noticer

You were the one who noticed
when my smile bent wrong,
when the light touched my face
but didn't reach my eyes.
You could hear it in my breath,
a thinness entering the room.

I wonder if it was love,
or something older.
The cord was cut,
yet our beat stayed shared.
Two hearts,
one rhythm.

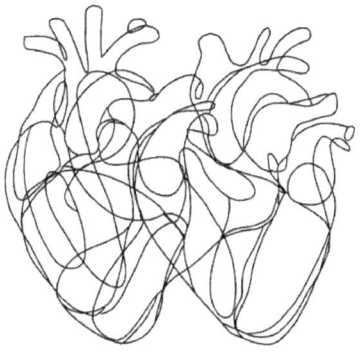

i had you in july

celebration

Plan a party.
Host it.
Cater it.
Post it in the paper.
Invite anyone.
You might know them,
you might not.
Will fifteen people come?
Two hundred fifteen?
You won't know until they do.
Stand there on display
while you are at your lowest,
your most vulnerable,
your saddest.
Call it
a celebration.

adrift

Untethered
I drift
A small boat lost to the tide
No compass
No anchor
Just the frayed rope
of what's left behind

i had you in july

sentinel

Sentinel
Sen·ti·nel
/ˈsentənəl/
 noun
A soldier.
A guard.
One whose job
is to stand and keep watch.

I wasn't.

five hours

I told you.
Ever since
after,
I look for pieces of you.

Everywhere,
I look for you.

I mean,
I want your grocery lists.
I want your recently saved images off your phone.
I want—

Oh.
Good idea.
I should open the recordings
from the front-door camera
and I can see you.
Beautiful you,
bumbling with the bumblebees
while you nourish your
incredible,
colorful
garden.

But instead

"Help."

I hear.
My body frozen,
yet hot knives
stab every cell.

This is
the day of.
10:00 AM.

I had just left you.
An hour ago
I had *just* left you.

And there you were
in my hands,
calling for help.

But
I didn't check the notification.

I
I
I could have come running home.

Or

Dad?
Dad.
Dad was home.

Didn't he see?
Didn't he hear

You.
You.
You could have used your watch,
your phone,
at any point to call,
to say,
I need help.

"I heard her," he trembled,
choking.
I ask him,
"She called for help?"
"I came to her.
She said her neck was really stiff,
I rubbed her neck,
and after about twenty minutes

she said she felt better."

A *sentinel leak*, they call it.

It can feel like
a bat
is hitting you
over the head.

But in a sentinel leak,
before the
full
rupture,
the brain can make a temporary repair.

Of course you would.
You would repair.
You always repaired.
We did.

I shift.

Dad didn't go to work that day.
And he always went to work.
But this time he stayed,
said you didn't seem right.
He wanted to look out for you.
Said you wanted to go driving,
to get back to being in the sun,
but he was worried,
told you not to drive, to stay inside the air conditioning.
He said you felt better,
started sorting through the
polymer clay earrings I made you,
the ones you love so much.

Until.
Until you started asking things like,

"Why aren't my toes working?"

as you sat on the bathroom floor,
soon to be unconscious.

Five hours from
A haunting video
frozen in time,
the ambulance would take you.

And I can't stop
cannot stop
wondering
if one of us had gotten to you sooner,
if we somehow just
could have
KNOWN,

could we have been
your sentinel?

before and after

There will always be a *before*,
when I had you,
and *after*,
where every moment
will forever
carry the weight
of missing you.

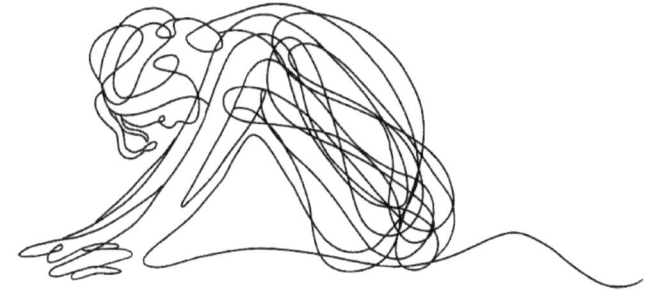

i had you in july

unfinished

I wasn't done loving you.
I wasn't done

american

We take months to welcome life.
We take days to bury it.

Books teach swaddles, first steps.

Who teaches us how to hold
emptiness?

Grief?
Grief is handled in private.
Oh, you're hurting?
Debilitated?
Cracked wide open?
Shh.
Tuck that shit in.
Get back to work.
Get back to life.

The expectation is to return
as if nothing happened.
But I can't.

Holding the ashes of my old life
in one hand,
and routine
with a pulse
in the other.

promises

Promise? His voice breaks.
Look at me. He pleads.
He wants me to promise him that I'll be okay.
That we'll get through this.
My eyes screaming what's too heavy to say,
how can I promise something I don't believe?

ordinary

Grief comes with me to the kitchen,
waits while I open the fridge,
follows me to the sink.
I set it at the table,
feed it leftovers,
wash it down with silence.

i had you in july

kintsugi

When I lost you,
I lost the kind of love
that stayed when my edges were sharp,
the kind that gathered my broken pieces
as if they were worth keeping,
believing they could become
something even more valuable
than gold.

fact or flight

Dad saw a butterfly and swore it was you.
He said, in all his 65 years,
he'd never had one fly into his truck.

I've always prided myself on being objective
clinging to empirical evidence,
refusing to let my thoughts drift too whimsical.

I used to like that about myself.

Until I realized it meant
I didn't leave space for wonder.
I didn't let myself believe in
signs.

Everything became just science,
human error,
coincidence,
reason after reason
to close the door.

And in doing so,
I have left no room
for the light to enter.

i had you in july

natural

They say losing a parent first
is the natural order of things.
But what if the parent you lost
still had so much life left to live?
What if their death was not gentle,
but
horrific,
catastrophic.
What if they had to suffer?
What if that person was your entire world,
and now the world feels unlivable,
so much so you find yourself wishing
you had gone with them?
They say it's the natural order of things
but nothing about this
feels natural
at all.

claws

My mind may try to distract me
from the silence of your absence,
but there is within me,
a guttural knowing,
a longing
that claws,
that tears through
every moment,
a constant throbbing in my bones.
It presses against my chest.
It does not rest.
My cells reverberate the echo of your making,
the wound of your leaving.

i had you in july

inheritance

"This one I've had
since before your sister was born."
"Oh, wow," I scrolled my phone.

I hardly looked up,
but I should have.
I didn't ask,
but I should have.

Now the forest is mine.
Half a century of green.

What do I do?

They live on without you.
I want to hate them.
I want to hold them.

all that fades was gold

Her hands grew these blooms.
I dry them for weeks, press them flat,
teach them how to stay.
I pour resin the way she poured love.
I work quickly.
I must save them
before the marigolds
surrender their gold.
Nature does not wait.

i had you in july

the cost of understanding

"HoLd YoUr LoVeD oNeS cLoSe."

They told me, too.
And I thought I understood.
You Fool.
I hear myself laugh
for the first time in weeks.

Only to realize that to
truly understand
the

silence

where your laughter
used to
live
is to be forced to
live
without it.

farther

Forty-seven days.
Each one pulling me
farther from your voice.

I tell myself,
this is the nearest I'll ever be.

But time is merciless.
Grief steals pieces,
blurs the edges.

When was it?
Our last hug?

Your warmth
is alive,
not just remembered.

i had you in july

hollow

I screamed until I was
raw,
surprised at
the quiet
faint echo that
even my loudest screams held.

That was *it?*
I didn't rattle the picture frames,
didn't loosen the nails in the wall,
didn't even wake the dust.

This rage
inside me,
this
all-encompassing
ache,
feels like it could
collapse this
whole
hollow
house.

what i cannot do

Throw away the frozen protein drink
you left in the freezer.
Move the Tajín you set beside me
with a boiled egg that morning,
so I wouldn't get sick.

I'm saving your tomato seeds.
I don't even like tomatoes.
Maybe one day I'll want to garden.
Today I can't stand the sun.

I can't find enough pieces of you.
Your journals are empty,
no letters titled
HOW TO LIVE WITHOUT ME.

I cannot make it through a single day
without weeping.
Step back into the office
where I was once a therapist
with steadier hands.
Escape the flashback
of your breath stopping at 9:37,
the clock's hands freezing
alongside yours.
Hold my father
without fearing the hour
he too will vanish.
Power down your cell phone,
still carrying your voice.

Carry this body,
as if it isn't missing half.

i had you in july

gold

I scour every corner of my phone.

Gold.
A video of me saying *I love you*
and you saying it back.

Back in your room,
I rip through your possessions.

Your wooden
treasure chest
of memories.
I open it,
unsure of its contents,
certain of its worth.

The first book stings.
All the wrong memories.
Why did we need fifty photos
in a book of Disney on Ice, 1994?
What I would give for fifty photos
in a book of you.

Gold.
I find a photo of you
giving me my first birthday cake.

Gold.
One photo of you pregnant with me.

Gold.
A flimsy paper
"award" I made
you saved it,
"#1 Mom."

I reach the bottom of the treasure chest
and my heart sinks.
I beg for more gold,

but there isn't.
There never will be.

I clutch what I have
paper thin scraps,
as light as paper,
as heavy as gold.

The riches I beg for,
no chest could hold them anyway.

i had you in july

overboard

I found fifteen-year-old me
writing from summer camp,
tucked inside your wooden chest.

The ink on the page addressed to
Mom.

I wrote *be safe*
into every goodbye letter,
my pen carving
quiet prayers.

"If you walked the plank,
I'd walk it too."

Because what I always
feared most,
wasn't losing myself,
it was losing you.

salty

Me and grief walk into the room,
she takes the bigger chair,
the one closest to you,
though nobody invited her.
Pass the salt? She asks.
I do.
She seasons everything.

i had you in july

if i could

A childhood with no shelter,
a life of labor.

You carried your pain,
then mine.

If I could go back,
I would place only love
in your arms
where the world left its weight.

If I could go back
I would rewrite the hours,
turn silence into questions,
sharpness into care.

If I could go back
I would show you a daughter
who learned sooner
how to love without fear.

If I could go back.

empty house

Coffee or tea?
Left or right?
Here or there?

Doesn't matter.

Same hand.
Same shuffle.
Same nothing.

Our deck is stacked.

i had you in july

poppy breath

How many would it take?
I type the question.
The answer
less than I imagined.

The bottle I hold is
light but
the contents heavy,
whispering
enough.

I break one in half and
close the lid.
This half will barely touch,
the aching, fractured, swollen,
abandoned tooth.
I let it dissolve,
a stand-in for weeks of forgetting
to care.

The house hums with emptiness.
So do I.

posttraumatic stress disorder (F43.11)

Panic grips my chest.
Vision blurred by tears.
The breath won't come,
only that **sound**,
that same awful sound you made
when you couldn't breathe.
I gasp for air as memory floods,
pulling me under.

keep her

I found something.
I am my Mother's Keeper.
It sat between us,
a sealed envelope
I never sent
but carried everywhere.

I asked you why,
how,
something?
But you didn't have an answer. Just a plea.

I stood there
holding something
I couldn't ever put down.
A tether, a vow,
a silence I kept for you.
For both of you.
And even now, I wonder if carrying the weight of that,

was my loudest love of all.

exfoliate

I see your uneasiness
at the presence of my sorrow,
hovering distantly,
waiting for the pain to shrink.
But this grief clings to me
like a second skin,
and I can't shed it
just to make you more comfortable.
Maybe you could sit with me here,
while I try to scrub away
this heaviness.

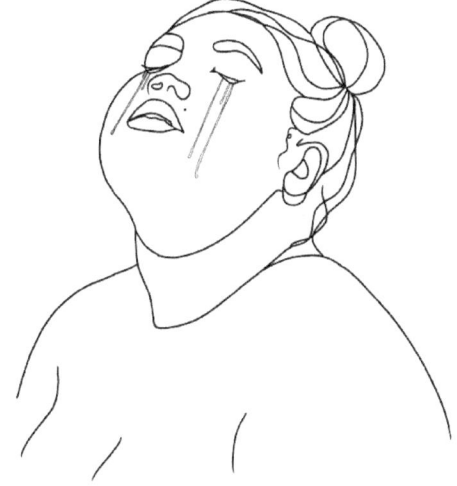

i had you in july

abundant

Your love was enough
for a lifetime
I just wish it didn't
have to be.

obscured

Everything is distorted.

Time ticks sideways,
slow and heavy.

Colors are too bright.
The sun is stabbing,
not warming.

Music is dissonant,
out of tune.

Laughter arrives metallic, clanging,
a faint echo from another life.

My hands move but never
quite touch what they
reach for.

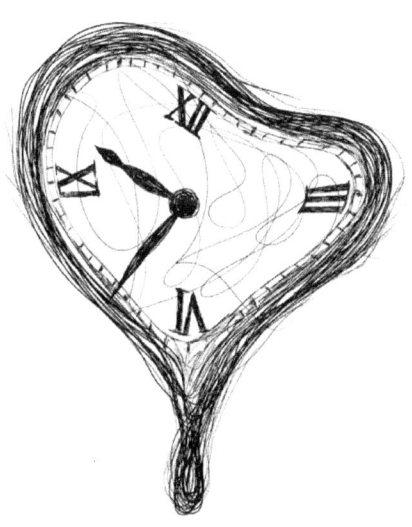

i had you in july

don't fall

My favorite season's almost here.
I used to curse the weight of summer,
relentless heat.
But grief rewrote my calendar.
Now I beg summer to stay
the leaves not to fall,
the world not to turn.
Because I am stuck
in your season,
the one where I last held you.

migration

The hummingbirds are leaving.
Your best friend comes daily
to fill the fifteen feeders you left behind,
a ritual of care
in your absence.

They don't circle as they did
when you were here,
but they still come.

Soon they'll leave,
tiny bodies remembering
the way south.
It shouldn't be possible
for something so small.
Yet they go.

I don't think I want them to go.
Their presence
in the spot you used to fill.
Another season
to echo the silence,
to magnify our distance.

The hummingbirds and I both
journey
them in open skies,
me in hollow dark.
Both of us go on
without you.

i had you in july

national hummingbird day

They came
carrying pieces of her life,
sharing them,
reminding me
her light has not stopped shining.

To my surprise
I had moments of
joy…
A word repeatedly used to describe you,
"Special."
Yes. You were.
You are special.

We gathered,
hummingbirds everywhere
on seed packets,
in the guest book,
at the tables.
Bedazzled hummingbird
pins intentionally adorned
the closest friends and family
who had stood through
twenty-one hospital days.

And then I learned
the very day we chose
without knowing,
without planning
was
National Hummingbird Day.

petals

Each petal,
a memory of your hands.
We water your flowers.
Your garden insists
though I resist,
that life goes on.

i had you in july

Acknowledgements

Daddy — Thank you for being forever steady, forever mine. I'd choose you in every lifetime. Mom gave me the taco recipe; I promise I'll make them for you.

Sissy — My best friend and constant. We carried what couldn't be carried, together. I'm so grateful you're in my corner. I love you.

Katelyn — You made sure I ate, slept (with a fan), showered, and laughed. You stayed with Mom so I could rest, hauled laundry, drove back and forth, and held me up for 21 days. I love you endlessly.

Deb — My Mom's longtime best friend. Thank you for watering her flowers, filling the feeders, keeping her memory alive, and loving her so well.

To the circle that showed up, Hannah, Marcie, Ashley, Debby, Josh, Rachel, Kallie, Brenda, Gram, Julia, Will, Sylvia, Tyler, Haley, Sarah, Ted, Shirley Jean, Cheri, Matthew, Jayden, Kamryn, Dan, Jennifer, Katy, Joey, Delaney, JJ, thank you for standing with us when we needed you most.

To the University of Iowa teams, neurosurgeons, doctors, nurses, CNAs, techs, MedFlight crew, and every person who cared for my Mom, thank you for your skill and your kindness.

To the Iowa Donor Network, thank you for the dignity, tenderness, and care you extended.

To my clients and my supervisor, Paula, thank you for your steady understanding and patience while I make room for grief and for healing.

Resources

If you are grieving, in crisis, or supporting someone through loss, these resources may offer comfort, community, or immediate help.

For medical emergencies in the U.S., call 911.

Crisis & Mental Health Support (U.S.)
• 988 Suicide and Crisis Lifeline: Call or text 988, or use webchat at 988lifeline.org for free, confidential support 24/7.
• Crisis Text Line: Text HOME to 741741 to connect with a trained crisis counselor.

Grief Support & Bereavement
• The Compassionate Friends: compassionatefriends.org
• Modern Loss: modernloss.com
• National Alliance for Children's Grief (NACG): nacg.org (formerly childrengrieve.org)
• Hospice Foundation of America: hospicefoundation.org
• GriefShare: griefshare.org

Outside the U.S., check your country's health ministry website for crisis lines and local grief organizations.

When Supporting Someone Grieving:
• Keep showing up. Grief is long. The "firsts" (birthdays, holidays, anniversaries) can be the hardest. Set reminders now.
• Say their loved one's name.
• Offer specific help. For example: "I'll bring dinner at 6," or "I'll walk the dog this week."
• Drop care without strings. Food, flowers, paper goods, leave them without expecting thanks.
• Listen, don't fix. Ask: "Do you want company, distraction, or quiet?"
• Invite gently. Keep it low-pressure, with an easy "no."

You are not alone in this.

Designed with love in memory of Shirley Ann.